D1710084

Little People, **BIG DREAMS**™

DWAYNE JOHNSON

Written by
Maria Isabel Sánchez Vegara

Illustrated by
Lirios Bou

Frances Lincoln
Children's Books

Once, a little boy named Dwayne was born into a family of wrestlers. His grandmother was a wrestling promoter and both his father and grandfather were famous champions. Still, he dreamt of becoming a hero in his own way.

Dwayne grew up wrestling with his father and working out next to his beefy buddies. But being the son of a wrestler meant he never stayed in one place for long.

Every time the family settled somewhere and Dwayne made friends, it was time to move on again!

He was a teen when his family lost almost everything they had. Dwayne felt hopeless and alone. The only thing he could control was his body, so he pushed himself to get fitter and stronger.

He won a scholarship to play football at college and even made it to the Canadian professional league.

But after two months,
Dwayne was cut from the team. Suddenly, he was back
at his parents' house with just a few dollars in his pocket.

He fell into a depression, an illness that made him very sad. The day he dared to ask for help, he realized that strong guys are not those with the biggest biceps, but those brave enough to accept their own weakness and open up to others.

Maybe his football career was over, yet Dwayne was ready to keep working hard! If he couldn't be a footballer, he would be the greatest performer on a stage that felt like home to him: the wrestling ring. All he had to do was practice day and night.

The day he stepped out from behind the curtain as Rocky Maivia, the first third-generation wrestler at the WWE, Dwayne looked like a star, but... somehow, the fans couldn't care less.

Soon, they were booing him even when he was winning a match!

Dwayne learned that winning in the ring didn't make a wrestler great. What really mattered was thrilling the audience. He needed to look inside himself and find a true hero who could hook the fans. And he did!

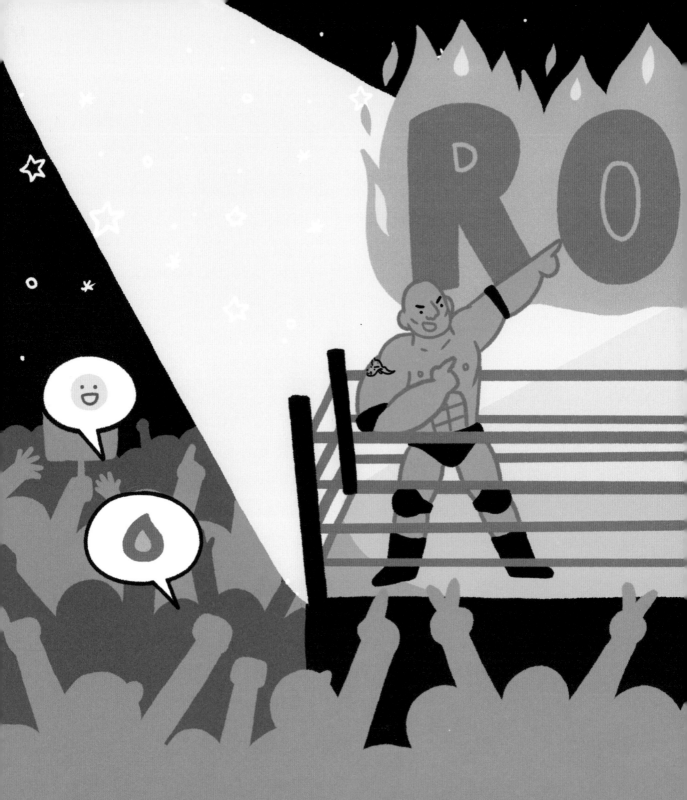

As The Rock, Dwayne became the wrestling legend he had longed to be: The People's Champ! He won many titles …

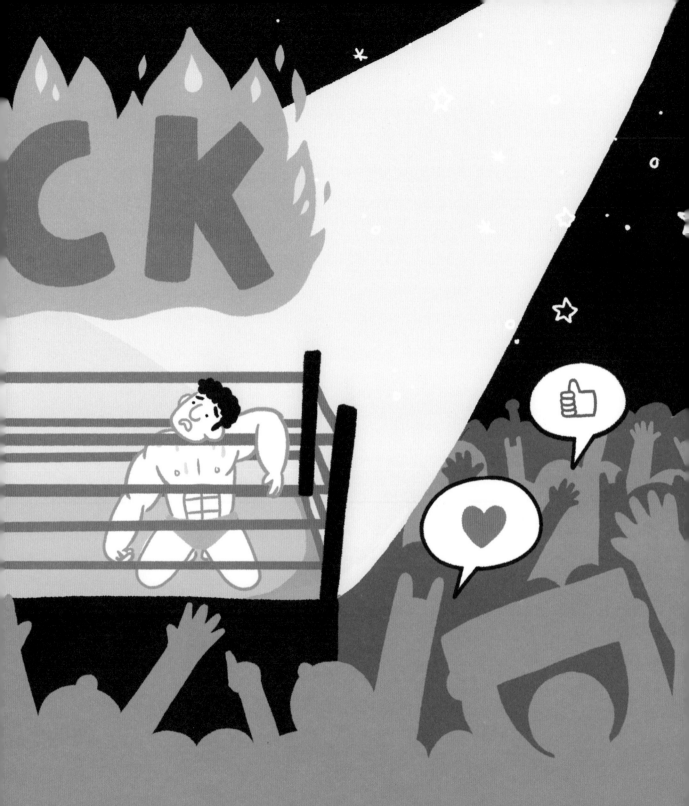

... but it was his magnetic personality that captured the fans' hearts. Soon, even Hollywood was knocking at his door.

He was offered the role of an evil Egyptian mummy in a movie that was an instant blockbuster. Yet, Dwayne didn't want to play the nasty dude, but the fearless guy ready to save the world with his big muscles and an even bigger heart.

Whether he played an anti-poaching ranger, a secret agent, or a rescue pilot, Dwayne had one single rule: there was no place for sad endings in his movies. He wanted everyone to have the feeling that good always wins.

Besides being the best-paid actor ever, Dwayne became a proud father and the co-founder of an entertainment company called Seven Bucks. Yet, he never stopped being a humble guy ready to inspire others with his enthusiasm.

And despite his fame, he still puts in the hard work, waking up before sunrise to train and plan his day. Because there will always be more dreams for little Dwayne to achieve, as long as he keeps being the most powerful thing he can be: himself.

DWAYNE JOHNSON

(Born 1972)

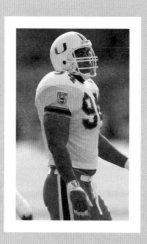

1994

2000

Dwayne Douglas Johnson was born in California, USA, to a family
of wrestlers. His father, Rocky "Soulman" Johnson, and grandfather,
Peter Maivia, were both professionals in the business. As a kid, Dwayne
would spend time on the road with his parents, accompanying them to
wrestling matches. After school, he earned a full scholarship from the
University of Miami to play football and, after graduating, he signed with
the Calgary Stampeders as a line-backer. But injuries led to him being cut
from the team just two months into the season and his football career came
to an abrupt end. Dwayne decided to follow in his family's footsteps and
made a name for himself as a professional wrestler. He pushed himself
with a gruelling training schedule, and soon Dwayne made his

2018   2021

WWE (World Wrestling Entertainment) debut as Rocky Maivia—a name that paid tribute to his father and grandfather. At first, he wasn't popular with fans, but after he changed his style and began to call himself The Rock, he became a hit with the audience and his life was transformed. Dwayne won 17 WWE titles across his career and became known as "The People's Champion." His career in Hollywood exploded after he was asked to star in his own movie, *The Scorpion King.* Since then, he has appeared in many much-loved movies and TV shows, including *Jumanji: Welcome to the Jungle, Moana,* and many more. A groundbreaking athlete and cinema superstar, Dwayne's life shows us that with talent, hard work, and determination, no dream is impossible to reach.

Want to find out more about **Dwayne Johnson?**

Have a read of this great book:

Who is Dwayne "The Rock" Johnson? by James Buckley Jr

Brimming with creative inspiration, how-to projects, and useful information to enrich your everyday life, quarto.com is a favorite destination for those pursuing their interests and passions.

Text © 2022 Maria Isabel Sánchez Vegara. Illustrations © Lirios Bou 2022.
Little People Big Dreams and Pequeña&Grande are registered trademarks of Alba Editorial, SLU for books, publications and e-books. Produced under licence from Alba Editorial, SLU.
First Published in the USA in 2022 by Frances Lincoln Children's Books, an imprint of The Quarto Group.
Quarto Boston North Shore, 100 Cummings Center, Suite 265D, Beverly, MA 01915, USA
Tel: +1 978-282-9590, Fax: +1 978-283-2742 www.Quarto.com

A catalogue record for this book is available from the Library of Congress.
ISBN 978-0-7112-8155-4
Set in Futura BT.

Published by Peter Marley • Designed by Sasha Moxon
Edited by Lucy Menzies and Claire Saunders • Production by Nikki Ingram
Editorial Assistance from Rachel Robinson
Manufactured in Guangdong, China CC062022
1 3 5 7 9 8 6 4 2

Photographic acknowledgements (pages 28-29, from left to right): 1. OCTOBER 22: Defensive end Dwayne Johnson #94 of the University of Miami Hurricanes walks on the field during the NCAA game against the University of Virginia on October 22, 1994. Dwayne Johnson is also known as "The Rock" of World Wrestling Federation. © Jed Jacobsohn via Getty Images. 2. World Wrestling Federation's Wrestler Rock Poses June 12, 2000 In Los Angeles, Ca. © Stringer via Getty Images 3. Dwayne Johnson, "Jumanji - Welcome to the Jungle," UK Premiere, Vue West End, London.UK . © Michael Melia via Alamy Stock Photo. 4. LOS ANGELES, CALIFORNIA, USA - NOVEMBER 04: Actor Dwayne Johnson arrives at the World Premiere Of Netflix's 'Red Notice' held at the Xbox Plaza and Chick Hearn Court at L.A. Live on November 4, 2021 in Los Angeles, California, United States. © Xavier Collin/Image Press Agency via Alamy Images

MIX
Paper from responsible sources
FSC® C008047

Collect the *Little People*, **BIG DREAMS**™ series:

FRIDA KAHLO	**COCO CHANEL**	**MAYA ANGELOU**	**AMELIA EARHART**	**AGATHA CHRISTIE**	**MARIE CURIE**	**ROSA PARKS**	**AUDREY HEPBURN**
EMMELINE PANKHURST 	**ELLA FITZGERALD**	**ADA LOVELACE** 	**JANE AUSTEN** 	**GEORGIA O'KEEFFE** 	**HARRIET TUBMAN** 	**ANNE FRANK** 	**MOTHER TERESA** 
JOSEPHINE BAKER	**L. M. MONTGOMERY** 	**JANE GOODALL** 	**SIMONE DE BEAUVOIR** 	**MUHAMMAD ALI** 	**STEPHEN HAWKING** 	**MARIA MONTESSORI** 	**VIVIENNE WESTWOOD**
MAHATMA GANDHI	**DAVID BOWIE** 	**WILMA RUDOLPH** 	**DOLLY PARTON** 	**BRUCE LEE** 	**RUDOLF NUREYEV** 	**ZAHA HADID** 	**MARY SHELLEY**
MARTIN LUTHER KING JR.	**DAVID ATTENBOROUGH** 	**ASTRID LINDGREN** 	**EVONNE GOOLAGONG** 	**BOB DYLAN** 	**ALAN TURING** 	**BILLIE JEAN KING** 	**GRETA THUNBERG**
JESSE OWENS	**JEAN-MICHEL BASQUIAT** 	**ARETHA FRANKLIN** 	**CORAZON AQUINO** 	**PELÉ** 	**ERNEST SHACKLETON** 	**STEVE JOBS** 	**AYRTON SENNA** 
LOUISE BOURGEOIS	**ELTON JOHN** 	**JOHN LENNON**	**PRINCE** 	**CHARLES DARWIN** 	**CAPTAIN TOM MOORE** 	**HANS CHRISTIAN ANDERSEN** 	**STEVIE WONDER**

MEGAN RAPINOE

MARY ANNING

MALALA YOUSAFZAI

ANDY WARHOL

RUPAUL

MICHELLE OBAMA

MINDY KALING

IRIS APFEL

ROSALIND FRANKLIN

RUTH BADER GINSBURG

MARILYN MONROE

KAMALA HARRIS

ALBERT EINSTEIN

CHARLES DICKENS

YOKO ONO

MICHAEL JORDAN

NELSON MANDELA

PABLO PICASSO

AMANDA GORMAN

GLORIA STEINEM

FLORENCE NIGHTINGALE

HARRY HOUDINI

J.R.R. TOLKIEN

ELVIS PRESLEY

NEIL ARMSTRONG

ALEXANDER VON HUMBOLDT

NIKOLA TESLA

WILMA MANKILLER

MARCUS RASHFORD

LAVERNE COX

MAE JEMISON

DWAYNE JOHNSON

HELEN KELLER

ACTIVITY BOOKS

STICKER ACTIVITY BOOK

COLORING BOOK

LITTLE ME, BIG DREAMS JOURNAL

Discover more about the series at www.littlepeoplebigdreams.com